STARLIGHT INYAMA

Rich Life
Realized

How to Get Rich and Be Happy in Your Personal Life for a Long, Happy Life

STARLIGHT

Starlight Inyama

DEDICATION

This work is dedicated to God Almighty, for His mercies and goodness.

Table of contents

Chapter 4
Navigating Challenges and Setbacks
Developing Resilience and Overcoming
Obstacles in the Goal of Achievement

Chapter 5
Generosity and Giving Back
What Does Giving Back Mean To You:
Exploring the Impact of Generosity
The Benefits of Giving Back
Ways to Give Back to Your Community
Giving Back Quotes & Inspiration for
Generosity
The Ripple Effect of Giving Back: Impact
Beyond the Individual
The Power of Inspiration
Giving Back Activities: Creating Opportunities
for Generosity
Encouraging Generosity in the Workplace
The Joy of Giving Back

Mastering the Financial Mindset

How to Think Like a Rich Person to Be Successful

There are too many people today who think that only very rich people who can hire an accountant can understand their finances and make a plan to progressively increase their wealth.

But here's the truth: anyone can adopt a wealth mindset that allows them to earn, save, and build the future they want without losing their happiness or family time in the present. It doesn't matter how much money you make.

Sound too good to be true? Developing a wealthy attitude is the first step, and here's what you need to get started.

What is a Wealth Mindset?

Managing your money wisely is about more than just crunching the numbers to see if you can meet financial goals. A wealth attitude is the basis of all of your buying and saving habits, and it starts with the psychology of money.

You need to ask yourself the real questions and be honest with yourself about the solutions. What is your first sense of money? How does it feel to spend your hard-earned cash? What is your mental link to money? Are there any preconceived ideas you have about wealth and how to grow it?

Wealth attitude is often passed from your family of origin, and it can grow through your situations with money. A healthy attitude has a huge effect on your general financial success, along with information and actions to back it up.

Strategies to Develop a Wealth Mindset

How can you create a strong wealth mindset? It might be easier than you think. If you're ready to start focusing on how you can improve your thinking when it comes to wealth building, here's where to start.

1. Understand Your Behavior

Before you can start building more wealth, you need to understand where your money is going to begin with.

That's right. We're talking about the feared B-word: your budget.

Understanding how you spend your money is only the first step. You also need to dig deep into the feelings that surround your spending. How does it feel to spend your money? Does every single one of your purchases make you feel stressed to the max? Are you spending money for short-term stress release, even though it makes you more worried later in the month?

With a handle on your emotional reaction to spending, you can start to tease out what needs to happen next to help you set goals.

2. Set Goals

Once you know where your money is going and get a grip on the connection between spending and your feelings, it's time to start setting goals.

Goal-based financial planning aims to set clear and doable steps to reach your goals. It is more detailed than a few vague ideas such as "saving for retirement" though.

Instead, a goal-based financial plan is super specific and gives you real steps to take to provide direction for your future. To build your wealth attitude, you should know where you need to go to get to those big dreams you have. You'll be able to achieve your dreams with less fear and more financial security when you conquer this skill.

3. Focus on the Positives

The opposite of a wealth mindset is a shortage mindset, and many people fall into this trap when it comes to handling their money.

Making choices based solely on fear will hold you back from achieving your goals. Instead of focusing on fear, try to find positive angles by looking for chances, answers, and steps you can take right now.

In other words, you should look ahead rather than behind you.

Keep in mind that even debt can be a good thing, though we are often told the opposite of this idea. Think of it this way: someone else (the bank) is tying up their resources (money) to hold your mortgage or loan. This means that your money can be spent elsewhere — ideally at a better rate of return than the interest you pay on the debt itself.

See how easy it can be to focus on the positives, even in situations that you might have originally thought of as negatives?

4. Free Up Your Time

There's no way around it: your time is important, and you aren't the best at everything.

Instead of spending endless hours trying to accomplish the things that you're bad at, you can free up some of your own time (and valuable energy and money) by paying an expert to do those items on your to-do list.

With all that freed-up time, you can spend your time making more money. Develop yourself or your skills, and take on extra clients — whatever the case may be. This eventually earns you more money and makes up for the cash you spent paying someone else. Investing your time in the areas where you're best is crucial to building wealth.

5. Find a Mentor or Advisor You Can Trust

Many people who know they want to save for the future are quick to hire an accountant or some other type of professional to help them get there. Financial managers are a great addition to your team and they can ask the hard questions about where your money is going and whether that fits with your goals.

But the goal shouldn't be to find someone who just crunches the numbers for you. Instead, focus your efforts on finding someone who will offer advice, teach you, and help you to understand and improve your attitude.

That might mean an expert who offers support or shares new methods for success. And yes, sometimes even a planner who's honest enough to say it straight and talk you out of that not-so-smart business idea.

Ways To Build A Healthy Relationship With Money

A good relationship with money is all about our actions. Your financial goals and how you spend your money are determined by your habits, thoughts, and feelings about money.

Of course, you already know that you should spend less than you make. That's the first rule when it comes to personal spending. But sometimes our mind can play tricks on us and change the way we think about money.

If you've tried to achieve a tough goal before and failed, you know that it takes a lot more than just following a step-by-step plan. It comes down to your attitude.

Here are a few tips to help improve your money thinking so you can start taking an active part in building your wealth. These tips will help you build a good relationship with money if you want to be rich!

1. Money is a tool

Back when I was in college, I used to say things like "I wish I had more money" or "I need to save money".

To be honest, I didn't have a good relationship with money and kept treating it as a goal. I used to think that having more money would solve all of my issues. But in fact, money is just a tool.

Once I made this mindset shift, I was able to focus on the result of my actions, instead of my positive or negative feelings towards money. Money itself is not the goal – it's a tool I can use to help me achieve my goal (pay for college, travel more, and so on). This new way of thinking also helped me to avoid spontaneous buying.

Just because I had this attitude shift, it didn't mean that my money problems vanished overnight. Going forward, it helped me to take care of my earnings and be more thoughtful about the way I spend and use my money. It helped me to build a better relationship with money.

Action Step: Ask yourself what it means to you (what do you need the money for) and set your spending goals accordingly. For example, I like going out to eat, but I love traveling. Understanding that money is a tool helps me to spend my money wisely (spend less at restaurants) so I can do more of what I love (traveling).

2. Don't sweat the small stuff

Back when I started learning how to save money, I used to pinch pennies and worry about small costs such as having to pay more money for brand-name goods when the generic brand was out of stock.

Since I set spending goals, it's helped me to not sweat the small stuff when it comes to money. Now I focus on the big wins.

For example, when I was working at my first real job after college, I was making $38,000 per year and spent all of my energy on cutting out daily coffee, tracking my spending, and doing all the usual personal finance tips.

While these saving habits stuck with me over the years, it took me a long time to save enough money to manage to attend graduate school. Plus, I used to feel nervous whenever I spent money (even on things I needed) because I was so focused on the small stuff.

My income stayed stable at my job, so I spent the majority of my energy on saving money. The shortage attitude was very real for me. I was afraid of never having enough and finding ways to make extra money wasn't on my mind at that time.

Fast forward a few years later, I started focusing on the big wins. Even though I used my savings to pay for graduate school, I started a side hustle that nearly tripled my income. This allowed me to rebuild my savings in less than a year and continue to set spending plans that matched my goals. Instead of thinking about spending $3 on a latte once in a while, I focused on finding ways to increase my income and do more things that made me happy.

Now I spend 70% of my energy on income-generating and health tasks, and I spend 30% of my energy on saving money. This helped me to build a good bond with my funds.

Action Step: Create a plan that values tasks that create income and bring you joy. Focus on the big wins, because at the end of the day, you can only save so much money, but there is no limit to how much you can make.

3. Wealth is a mindset

If you want to be rich, you need to create the right attitude. That's what this whole blog post is about!
Rarely will any millionaire tell you that their wealth came from a single job or investment. Instead, what most rich people will tell you is

that the key to their success is having a "millionaire mindset".

So many people believe that they'll never get out of debt or break the cycle of living paycheck to paycheck because they think that's just a way of life today.

This isn't true, most of these millionaires made their wealth themselves. They didn't have a helping hand and waited around for Prince Charming to come and save them – they went out and made their chances. They took control of their money.

Action Step: The first step in building the right money attitude to grow your wealth is to get clear on what you need the money for, which we covered in point #1.

The second step is to get rid of your limiting views about money, which are currently holding you back from getting what you want (your end goal). This will allow you to build a good relationship with money so you can use it as a tool to achieve your end goal.

4. Live like you're broke

Living like you're broke simply means living a cheap lifestyle (no matter what your income level is) so you can save for the really important things, such as spending your money.
When it comes to personal finance though, the way we choose to handle our money is unique.

For example, I can be quite cheap for some things. I make my cleaning products, I cook the majority of my food from scratch, I pay under $10 per month for my cell phone plan, I don't buy new clothes unless I need something, and I don't have cable TV.
On the other hand, I like to save a part of my pay so I can go to shows, travel, and invest my money. When I was growing up, I don't remember any of the material stuff my parents bought me. But I have happy memories of our yearly family trips together. These are the moments that I cherish most and that's why I save money so I can afford to make new memories.

As my salary grew, my buying habits stayed the same. I still live frugally so I can save money for the things that are important to me.

Action Step: Save your money to spend! While saving money to afford travel is fun, you also want to make sure that you're saving your money to spend. Investing your money is the key to building your wealth.

5. Control your feelings

How do you feel about money? Do you feel shame, fear, or anger?

If you answered "yes" to any of these thoughts, you're not alone. These are the most common feelings surrounding money.

If we have bad thoughts about money, chances are we'll always experience money troubles. On the other hand, if we have good thoughts about money, we're more likely to think that money is within our control.

These good feelings will also push us to teach ourselves about money so we can increase our income and be smart with how we handle our money.

Removing these bad thoughts about money can help us beat our money blocks so we can change our financial situation and build a better relationship with money.

We can't always control our financial problems but, we can still decide how we'll meet them. You have the choice to take control of your money. It's time to own your saving and spending choices.

Building a good relationship with money is important if you want to grow your wealth (and be rich). Even if you just want to stop living salary to paycheck and afford to take a yearly holiday, having a good relationship with money is important to achieve that.

Choosing to change your attitude is the first step in changing your relationship with money.

The sooner you understand that money is not the goal, the sooner you'll find peace and be able to focus on what truly makes you happy.

Strategic Wealth Building

The Basic Concepts Of Creating Wealth

An important goal for many people is to get rich, but it can feel like an impossible job. Getting this goal done will take time, work, and focus, so don't fall for get-rich-quick plans or chances that seem too good to be true. They could lead you astray.

No matter your background, some rules and methods can help you get rich and keep it for a long time. And the earlier you start doing these things, the more likely it is that they will work.

Setting goals and making a plan, engaging in education and skills, handling debt, saving and spending, protecting your assets, knowing how taxes affect you, and building a strong credit history are some of the most important things you can do to get rich. We will talk more about each of these ideas and how they can help you reach your financial goals in this piece.

1. Make Cash

Start making money right away. This step might seem simple, but it's the most important one for people who are just starting. You may have seen graphs that show how a small amount of money saved regularly and allowed to grow over time can finally add up to a large amount. Is there a simple question that numbers don't answer? How do you save money in the first place?

You can make money in two main ways: through paid income or idle income. You get earned income from the things you do for a living, and you get passive income from savings. This kind of cash might not come in until you have enough money to start saving.
If you are about to start a new job or are thinking about switching careers, these questions might help you figure out what you want to do and where you will get your money:

(i). What do you like? Doing something you enjoy and find important will help you do better at work, build a job that lasts longer, and increase your chances of making money. One study found that more than nine out of 10 workers said they would trade a share of their career salary for greater meaning at work.

(ii) What are you good at? Look at what you do well and how you can use those skills to earn a living.

(iii) What will pay well? Look at jobs using what you enjoy and do well that will meet your cash goals. One good source of pay information, as well as the growth chances for different areas, is the yearly Occupational Outlook Handbook released by the U.S. Bureau of Labor Statistics.

(iv) How do you get there? Learn about the schooling, training, and experience standards needed to follow your chosen job choices. The Occupational Outlook Handbook has information on this, too.

Taking these factors into account can help put you on the right path.

A good way to improve your income potential is to invest in your schooling and skills. Getting higher academic degrees, industry-specific certifications, and training programs are all useful to build your human capital.

2. Set Goals and Develop a Plan

Setting goals is an important first step in building wealth. When you have a clear picture of what you want to achieve, you can create a plan that will help you get there.

Start by describing your financial goals, such as saving for retirement, getting a home, or paying off debt. Be clear about the amount of money you need to achieve each goal and the time frame in which you hope to achieve it.

Once you have set your goals, you should build a plan for meeting them. This may involve making a budget to help you save more money, growing your pay through schooling or job growth, or investing in assets that will increase in value over time. Your plan should be reasonable, fluid, and focused on the long run. Regularly check your work, and make changes as needed to keep yourself on track.

3. Save Money

Simply making money won't help you build wealth if you end up spending it all. Moreover, if you don't have enough money saved up for your near-term responsibilities (like bills, rent, or mortgage) or an emergency, then you should value saving enough above all else. Many experts suggest having several months' (e.g., three to six) worth of income saved up for such scenarios.

Consider making the following changes to increase your savings:

(i) Track your spending for at least a month.

You might want to use a financial software package to help you do this, but a small, pocket-size notebook could also serve. Record your every expense, no matter how small; many people are surprised to see where all their money goes.

(ii) Find the fat and trim it.

Break down your spending into needs and wants. Food, housing, and clothes are clear wants. Add health insurance payments to that list, along with auto insurance if you own a car and life insurance if other people are depending on your income. Many other spending will merely be wanted.

(iii) Set a savings goal.

Once you have a fair idea of how much money you can set away each month, try to stick to it. This doesn't mean that you have to live like a miser or be cheap all the time. If you're meeting your spending goals, feel free to treat yourself and splurge (a suitable amount) once in a while. You'll feel better and be inspired to stay on track.

(iv) Put saving on automatic.
One easy way to save a set amount each month is to plan with your company or bank to immediately move a certain part of every paycheck into a separate savings or investment account. Similarly, you can save for retirement by having money regularly taken from your pay and put into your employer's 401(k) or similar plan. Financial advisers generally suggest giving at least enough to get your employer's full matching payment.

(v) Find high-yield savings
Maximize the payoff of your savings by shopping for savings accounts that have the highest interest rates and lowest fees. Certificates of deposit (CDs) can be a good savings choice if you can afford to lock up that money for several months or years.
Keep this in mind, too: You can only cut so much in costs. If your costs are already down to

the bone, then you should look into ways to improve your income.

4. Invest

Once you've managed to set aside some money, the next step is spending it so that it will grow. Money put in savings is important, but the interest rates paid on bank accounts tend to be very low, and your cash risks losing buying power over time to inflation.

Perhaps the most important financial idea for newbies (or any investment, for that matter) is diversity. Simply put, your goal should be to spread your money among different types of stocks. That's because stocks perform differently at different times. For example, if the stock market is on a loss run, bonds may be giving good results. Or if Stock A is in a slump, Stock B may be on a tear.

Mutual funds provide some built-in diversity because they invest in many different stocks. And you'll achieve better diversity if you buy in both a stock fund and a bond fund (or several stock funds and several bond funds), for example, rather than in just one or the other. As another general rule, the younger you are, the more risk you can afford to take because you'll have more years to make up for any losses.

Types of Investments

Investments range in terms of risk and possible gain. As a general rule, the safer they are, the smaller their possible return, and vice versa. If you aren't already familiar with the different types of investments, it's worth spending a little time reading up on them. While there are all kinds of unusual options, most people will want to start with the basics: stocks, bonds, and mutual funds.

Stocks
Stocks are shares of ownership in a company. When you buy stock, you own a tiny part of that company and will gain from any rise in its share price, as well as any profits that it gives out.

Stocks are usually seen as riskier than bonds, but stocks can also vary greatly in risk from one company to another.

Bonds

Bonds are like IOUs from a company or government. When you buy a bond, the seller offers to pay your money back, with interest, after a certain time. As a very general rule, bonds are viewed as less dangerous than stocks, but with less possible gain. At the same time, some bonds are riskier than others; bond-rating companies give them letter grades to represent that.

Mutual funds

Mutual funds are groups of securities—often stocks, bonds, or a mix of the two. When you buy mutual fund shares, you get a slice of the total pool. Mutual funds also vary in risk, based on what they spend.

Exchange-traded funds (ETFs)

Exchange-traded funds (ETFs) are like mutual funds in that each share holds a full collection of securities, but ETFs are posted on markets and trade like stocks. Some ETFs track big stock markets like the S&P 500, particular business groups, or asset types like bonds and real estate.

Warning: Before you start spending, make sure you have sufficient funds and some money set aside to handle any sudden financial problems.

5. Protect Your Assets

You've worked hard to earn your money and grow your wealth. The worst thing could be to lose it all due to a quick loss or unexpected event. A fire can burn down your house, a car accident can cause damage and hospital bills, or premature death can mean a loss of future income.

Insurance is a key piece of building your wealth because it offers safety from these and other dangers. Home insurance will replace your home and goods in case of a fire, auto insurance will make you whole after a car accident, and life insurance will pay your children a death bonus in the case of an unexpected death. Long-term disability insurance is another type of coverage that will replace your income if you become hurt, sick, or otherwise helpless and unable to continue working. Even young, healthy people should consider insurance goods since they tend to become more expensive as you grow older. That means even if you are 25 years old and single, getting life insurance then could be a lot more cost-effective than when you are 10 years older with a partner, children, and debt.

6. Minimize the Impact of Taxes

Taxes are an often-overlooked drag on your wealth-building efforts. Of course, we are all subject to income tax and sales tax as we earn and spend money, but our savings and assets can also be taxed. That's why it is important to understand your tax issues and build tactics to reduce their effect.

One easy way to reduce your tax bill is to invest in tax-advantaged funds. These accounts, such as 529 college savings plans, individual retirement accounts (IRAs), and 401(k) plans, offer tax perks that can help you save more money and lower your tax bill. For example, contributions to a standard IRA or 401(k) are tax-deductible, meaning that you can lower your taxable income and save money on taxes in the year when you donate. Moreover, they grow tax delayed, meaning that when you leave and are more likely to be in a lower tax rate, the effects will be smaller. Investment gains in a Roth IRA or Roth 401(k) are tax-free, meaning that you can grow and remove money in a Roth account without paying taxes on any of the income or gains.

Another technique for reducing taxes is to be aware of the time and location of your purchases. By keeping assets for more than a year, you can take advantage of the lower long-term capital gains tax rate, which is usually lower than the short-term capital gains tax and income tax rates. You should also be aware of where certain assets are held. Given the choice, an income-producing asset like a dividend-paying stock or company bond should be put in a tax-advantaged account like a Roth IRA, where these payments will not cause taxable events. A growing company that will only produce capital gains (rather than income) might instead be better placed in a taxed account.

Working with a trained tax professional, such as a bookkeeper or a certified public accountant (CPA), can help you stay on top of these changes and build a tax plan that works for your unique financial position. By knowing the impact of taxes and building methods to reduce their impact, you can build wealth more effectively and keep more of your hard-earned money over the long run.

7. Manage Debt and Build Your Credit

As you build wealth, you'll start to find it useful to take on loans to pay for different purchases or investments. You may pay for things with a credit card to earn points or prizes. You might ask for a mortgage for a home or second home, a home equity loan for home improvements, or an auto loan to buy a car. Maybe you'll want to take out a personal loan to help start a business or invest in someone else's.

However, it's important to handle your debt carefully—taking on too much debt could slow your progress toward your wealth-building goals. To handle debt, be aware of your debt-to-income (DTI) percentage and make sure that your debt payments are manageable within your budget. You should also try to pay off high-interest debt, such as credit card debt, as quickly as possible to avoid paying excessive interest charges.

Be careful of changeable or flexible interest rate products like adjustable-rate mortgages (ARMs), or those with balloon payments, as changes to the market or your circumstances can quickly cause those bills to become overwhelming.
Indeed, if you fall into debt, your credit score can be badly affected, and if you fail on your bills, you could face personal bankruptcy.

8. Maintain a Good Credit Score

Building and keeping a good credit score is an important part of building and protecting your income over the long run. You'll enjoy a lower interest rate and better terms on your loans if you have a good credit background and high credit score, which can save you thousands of dollars in interest charges over time.

Here are a few key steps that you can take to keep a good credit score:

(i) Pay your bills on time.
One of the most important things that affects your credit score is your payment history. To keep a good credit score, you should make sure to pay your bills on time, every time. Late payments, even if they're only a few days late, can have a major bad effect on your credit score.

(ii) Keep your credit utilization low.
Your credit utilization, or the amount of credit you're using compared to the amount you have available, is another important factor that

affects your credit score. To maintain a good credit score, you should try to keep your credit utilization below 30% of your available credit.

(iii) Monitor your credit record.

It's a good idea to check your credit report regularly to make sure that all the information is correct and up to date. Today, several sites will provide you with a credit report free of charge. Errors on your credit report can negatively impact your credit score, so it's important to challenge any errors you find.

(iv) Avoid starting too many new accounts.

Every time you ask for credit, it can have a small bad effect on your credit score. To keep a good credit score, you should avoid starting too many new accounts in a short amount of time. Note, however, that if you do not use credit cards or don't have enough credit lines open, you may fall victim to not having a suitable credit background. So, open some credit cards and take out some loans, but do not overdo it.

By following these steps and having good credit habits, you can keep a good credit score and maximize your borrowing power over the long run.

Should I pay off the debt or invest?

If you have high-interest debt, such as many credit card charges, it usually makes sense to pay it off before you spend. Few businesses ever pay as much as credit cards charge. Once you've paid off your debt, move that extra money to savings and investments. Try to pay your credit card amount in full each month, whenever possible, to avoid owing interest in the future.

How much money do I need to buy a mutual fund?

Mutual fund companies have different minimum spending needs to get started, often beginning at about $500. After that, you can generally spend less. Some mutual funds will waive their original minimums if you promise to spend a regular sum each month. You can also buy mutual fund and exchange-traded fund (ETF) shares through a trading company, some of which charge nothing for starting an account.

What is an exchange-traded fund (ETF)? Exchange-traded funds (ETFs) are investment groups much like mutual funds. A key difference is that their shares are traded on stock markets (rather than bought and sold through a particular fund company). They sometimes charge cheaper fees as well. You can also buy them, along with stocks and bonds, through a trading company.

The ultimate conclusion
While get-rich-quick plans sometimes may be appealing, the tried-and-true way to build wealth is through regular saving and investing—and carefully allowing that money to grow over time. It's fine to start small. The important thing is to start and to start early. Earn money and then save and spend it smartly. Protect your belongings with insurance, and limit your tax risk.

Remember, building wealth is a path, not a goal. Celebrate your wins along the way, and don't get frustrated by failures or hurdles. With patience, focus, and a clear picture of your goals, you can achieve financial success and build wealth over the long run.

Life design for Fulfillment

How to Set and Reach Your Financial Goals

Your financial goals are your long-, short-, and medium-term plans for your money. Your ideas and personal goals should be in line with your cash goals. Financial goals are not the same as a budget or financial plan. They are clear, measured steps that, when taken, bring you closer to your dream future.

It's not up to luck to be financially successful; you have to set and work toward clear financial goals. Whether you want to retire in comfort, get out of debt, or visit the world, setting financial goals will help you accomplish your dreams.

What Are Your Money Goals?

Financial goals are specific aims you set for yourself when it comes to money. They all have something to do with different parts of your money. They range from short-term goals that meet your current needs and wishes to long-term dreams of what you want your financial future to look like.

Financial goals are not one-size-fits-all. They come in three different time frames: short-term (less than three years), mid-term (three to 10 years), and long-term (more than 10 years). Each type plays a unique role in your financial journey.

Financial Goal Time Frames

Short-Term
These relate to current wants or needs, such as home changes, dream trips, or emergency funds. Giving them specific and interesting names can improve drive.

Mid-Term
Mid-term or intermediate goals bridge the gap between short-term and long-term aims. Examples include improving your credit score and getting cash to start your own business.

They usually have a time range of three to 10 years and are stepping stones to bigger goals.

Long-Term

These include more faraway goals like getting a comfortable retirement or funding your grandchildren's schooling. Breaking down long-term goals into smaller, short-term, or mid-term steps ensures steady progress.

Your financial goals should match with your beliefs and plans for the future. As you set them, imagine the life you want to lead and how these goals fit into that picture.

In my time as a financial planner and financial guide, I've had the honor of working with clients from different backgrounds, covering various socioeconomic levels, relationships with money, neuro differences, and cultural views. What I've consistently noticed is that when it comes to matters of income, there's always going to be something on the goals list to address.

While the big, long-term goals are critical, especially for protecting one's financial future, it's equally vital to handle current wants and wishes or external factors like changing legislation that can impact one's financial environment.

My customers and I start on a trip to break down these lofty goals into doable, actionable steps. This method not only lowers the overwhelming nature of financial planning but also enables people to regain control and trust in their financial choices.

By handling both the broad and local parts of financial goals, my clients find the drive and focus they need to achieve their dreams.

Well-crafted financial goals are specific and smart:

(i) Specific: Goals should be clear and well-defined.

(ii) Measurable: What does growth look like? Examples of numbers include dollars, units, or events.

(iii) Attainable: Goals should be reasonable. Do you have the tools necessary to achieve this goal, such as time, skill, and cash capacity? Stretch goals are okay, but they shouldn't be out of reach.

(iv) Relevant: Will this goal help you achieve your main objective? Is this truly your goal or someone else's?

(v) Time-bound: When do you want to achieve this goal?
Start with broad goals and then make smart goals for them. Consider the steps involved on the road to achieving these goals and use these as the base.

Your Financial Goals and Your Budget Go Hand-in-Hand

Creating a realistic budget is an important step on the road to meeting your financial goals.

Your budget serves as a financial GPS, helping you maintain financial control and steer towards your desired places. It gives a clear view of your income, spending, and savings, allowing you to make smart financial choices.

Furthermore, a budget works as a conversation tool, especially in family funds. It can bridge the gap between different buying habits and goals among family members. By providing real data, you can explain the effect of financial decisions on everyone's goals, promoting better financial unity.

Benefits of Setting Financial Goals

Financial goals are the guide for your financial trip. When you achieve them, you're one step closer to making your financial dreams come true. Think of financial goals as the heart of your financial plan. They guide your financial choices, keep you on track, and lead you toward a more safe and successful future.

Concrete, written goals are easier to track and measure, keeping you inspired. Regularly reviewing your goals, budget, and financial concerns improves your financial control and reduces worry. It also helps you make informed decisions, ensuring your choices match with your goals.

Facing your financial situation head-on, having clear goals, and sticking to them can help ease this stress and provide a feeling of direction and financial security.

Tips for Setting Achievable Financial Goals

While goal setting is a key step in achieving financial success, I've often seen people face common mistakes that hinder their progress. Beyond the value of SMART goals, there are three basic roadblocks I've noticed time and again. In recognizing and managing these common challenges, you can open the way toward a more safe and successful financial future.

Common financial goal-setting pitfalls

1. Being in a Rush

Achieving financial goals is more similar to a run than a sprint. Attempting radical, fast changes can lead to being stressed, angry, and ultimately, failing in achieving your goals. In a world conditioned for quick results, it's important to accept patience and focus on steady, lasting changes.

2. Readiness for Change

Honesty with oneself is a crucial part of goal setting. While we may have big dreams, they must match our present mental, physical, and financial readiness. It's common to aim for great heights, but it's equally vital to ensure that these goals are realistic within your present circumstances.

3. Not Knowing Your "Why"

Many people set goals without stopping to think about their underlying reasons. It's important to ask yourself, "Why am I pursuing this goal?" What is the main force behind your cash aspirations? Is it to leave a long memory for your family or to ease the stress that comes from financial instability? Identifying your "why" and matching your goals with your core values can provide the necessary insight and drive to stay the course.

Tips for using financial thinking to reach your goals:

(i) Visualize your ideal life and identify financial goals that match this picture.
(ii) Give your goals names that conjure excitement and motivation.
(iii) Time-stamp your goals.
(iv) Create visual models to help you picture your goals.
(v) Automate your success.

This last tip can have a huge effect. Automating as many actions involved in moving toward your financial goals as possible can minimize the image that you're doing without or doing with less.

Fortunately, there is a wealth of tools available to automate and track your financial goals.

Resources for Setting and Reaching Financial Goals

Once you've set goals, you must track your success. Numerous tools can help you set and meet your financial goals, responding to different wants and preferences:

1. Budgeting Tools: Utilize tools like You Need A Budget (YNAB), Mint, or Quicken to build and control your budget.

2. Automated Saving: Apps like Acorns, Chime, and Digit can help you save regularly.

3. Online Banking Tools: Many banks offer online tools and records to watch your activities and accounts.

4. Financial tools: Access free tools and credit guidance services from groups like the National Foundation for Credit Guidance.

5. Government Resources: Government services like MyMoney.gov provide financial skills education and advice.

Remember, technology can be a powerful partner in meeting your financial goals. By scheduling key actions, you'll make progress without constant effort.

In addition to the valuable tool of automation, setting various forms of responsibility is important on your journey toward achieving your financial goals. Consider finding an accountability partner, someone who shares your financial goals and can offer support and motivation along the way. This person can act as a source of motivation when the going gets tough and can enjoy your wins with you. Social support can also be a vital resource, especially if you find that sharing your financial goals with friends or family helps keep you on track.

It's important to admit that despite your best efforts, not everything will unfold exactly as planned. Life is full of unexpected twists and turns, and financial journeys are no exception.

When faced with losses or unforeseen hurdles, remember to roll with the punches. Adaptability is a key trait of great goal-makers. Instead of focusing on what didn't go as expected, focus on how you can change your method and move forward.

Practice self-compassion throughout your financial journey. Be kind to yourself, especially when you face challenges. Avoid self-criticism and instead give understanding and kindness. Treat yourself with the same care you would give to a close friend facing a similar situation.

Lastly, when you do hit your financial milestones and achieve your goals, take a moment to enjoy your achievements. Rewarding yourself for your commitment and hard work can provide a well-deserved feeling of success and inspiration for future financial efforts. Remember, success in financial goal setting isn't just about getting the target; it's also about loving the trip and recognizing your growth along the way. So, go ahead and treat yourself – you've earned it!

Navigating Challenges and Setbacks

Developing Resilience and Overcoming Obstacles in the Goal of Achievement

In the case of success, difficulties are expected. Life often presents us with hurdles, setbacks, and surprising turns. However, the key to turning these obstacles into stepping stones toward our goals lies in our ability to build resiliency. Resilience is an amazing quality that allows individuals to bounce back from hardship, adapt to change, and grow through tough situations.

In this book, we will study the importance of resilience and how it can help us beat hurdles on our road to success. By adopting perseverance, we can turn obstacles into chances for growth and move forward with a fresh drive.

Understanding Resilience

Resilience is more than just coming back; it is the ability to withstand hardship and emerge stronger. It includes a mix of mental, social, and psychological strengths that allow us to survive through tough times. Resilient people hold an unshakable belief in their skills and are not discouraged by mistakes. They view obstacles as brief hurdles rather than insurmountable roadblocks.

Embracing a Growth Mindset

A growth attitude is a useful tool for building resilience. Embracing this attitude means knowing that skills and gifts can be developed through commitment and hard work. Instead of being discouraged by loss, those with a growth mindset see it as a chance to learn and improve. Cultivating a growth mindset helps us to face obstacles with a positive and engaged attitude, promoting resilience in the face of hardship.

Building Emotional Intelligence

Emotional intelligence is the ability to understand and control our feelings successfully. Resilient people are skilled at spotting their feelings, controlling their reactions, and keeping calm in tough situations. Emotional intelligence allows us to deal with stress, handle disagreements effectively, and make thoughtful choices during difficult times. By building emotional intelligence, we can build the mental strength needed to handle tough scenarios with grace and clarity.

Cultivating a Support System

No one can face problems alone. Building a strong support system containing friends, family, teachers, or peers is important for building resilience. A support network offers motivation, help, and a safe space to share experiences and seek advice. During tough times, having a support system can provide comfort and encouragement, telling us that we are not alone in our journey towards success.

Practicing Self-Care

Resilience thrives when we value self-care. Taking care of our physical, mental, and social well-being helps us to recover and stay mentally sharp in the face of difficulties. Engaging in activities that bring joy and relaxation helps reduce stress and builds an adaptable mindset. Regular exercise, appropriate rest, and caring hobbies add to a strong base of resilience, allowing us to overcome challenges with clarity and drive.

Building resilience is a changing journey that allows us to face obstacles and thrive in the quest for success. Embracing a growth attitude, growing emotional intelligence, and creating a support system are important building blocks for resiliency. By valuing self-care, we keep the mental and physical strength needed to face challenges with courage and positivity.

Remember, difficulties are chances in disguise, and each obstacle conquered brings us closer to our goals. Embrace the power of endurance, stay persistent, and start on the rewarding road toward success with confidence and drive.

Generosity and Giving Back

What Does Giving Back Mean To You: Exploring the Impact of Generosity

Giving back is a basic act of kindness that has a permanent effect on both people and groups. It includes helping others by sharing time, resources, skills, and information to make the world a better place. But what does giving back mean to you?

At its core, giving back means making a conscious effort to improve the lives of others by offering support, kindness, and care. It can take many forms, from working at a local shelter to giving money to a nonprofit cause. Regardless of how you choose to give back, the effect of giving can be deep.

The Benefits of Giving Back

Generosity is a basic act of kindness that has significant benefits for both the giver and the receiver. In this part, we will cover the reasons why giving back is important and the good effect it can have on people and groups.

The Positive Impact on Mental Health

Giving back has been shown to have a good effect on mental health, lowering worry and anxiety levels. When we give our time, money, or resources to help others, it provides a sense of joy and happiness that can improve our mood and provide a sense of purpose.

Studies have also shown that giving back can lead to a drop in sadness rates and an increase in self-confidence and self-esteem. In turn, this can lead to a more positive view of life, making us more adaptable in the face of challenges and difficulties.

Building Meaningful Relationships

Giving back can also help us build important relationships with others. When we give our time to a cause we are excited about, we often meet like-minded people who share our values and interests. This can lead to the creation of new friendships and improve current ties. Giving back can also help us build connections with people from various backgrounds and places, boosting kindness and understanding between different groups of people.

Creating a Sense of Purpose and Fulfillment

Participating in acts of kindness can also provide a sense of meaning and satisfaction in our lives. When we give back, we are adding to something bigger than ourselves, making a good effect on the world around us. This sense of purpose can be especially rewarding for those who may be feeling a lack of direction or purpose in their lives.

Overall, giving back has numerous benefits that stretch beyond the act itself. It can improve our emotional health, build important connections, and provide a feeling of purpose and satisfaction in our lives. In the next part, we will explore ways you can give back to your local society.

Giving Back to the Community: Making a Difference Locally

Giving back to the community can have a significant effect on the lives of those around us. Whether through acts of kindness, charity work, or supporting local businesses and groups, there are countless ways to make a positive change in your neighborhood or city.

It's easy to feel overwhelmed by the many problems facing our communities, but making a difference can start with small, focused acts. Consider starting with a simple act of kindness, such as helping a friend with food or picking up trash in your local park.

Ways to Give Back to Your Community

1. Volunteer at a neighborhood charity or non-profit group
2. Donate to a local food bank or shelter
3. Support local businesses by shopping locally
4. Participate in neighborhood events and projects
5. Mentor or teach area kids

6. Create a neighborhood garden or urban farm

By getting active in local projects, you can also build important connections with other members of the community. Building bonds with those around us can build a better sense of connection and purpose, leading to greater general well-being.

Through giving back to the community, we can also handle bigger social problems and work towards building a more just and fair world. By helping disadvantaged groups and fighting for policies that promote equality and justice, we can create a positive ripple effect that stretches far beyond our neighborhoods.

Giving Back Ideas: Innovative Ways to Give Back
Giving back is an amazing way to have a good effect on the world and those around you. Whether you're new to giving back or looking for fresh ideas, there are countless ways to make a difference in your neighborhood and beyond.

Volunteer Your Time

Volunteering is one of the most important ways to give back to your community. Consider giving your time to a neighborhood soup kitchen, animal shelter, or community farm. You can also find chances to help at events or with local groups through websites like VolunteerMatch.org.

Support Small Businesses

Small businesses are the backbone of many towns, and helping them is a great way to give back. Consider shopping at local businesses instead of big-box stores, or visiting farmer's markets and craft shows to support local artists.

Donate to Charity

Charitable groups depend on gifts to fund their projects and make a change in the world. Research groups that match your ideals and consider giving to their cause. You can also set up regular payments to provide ongoing help.

Participate in a Fundraiser

Fundraisers are a fun way to give back while also meeting with others. Consider joining in a charity walk or run, or planning your fundraiser to help a cause you care about.

Offer Your Skills

Consider offering your skills to those in need. If you're a visual artist, offer to make marketing materials for a local charity. If you're a writer, offer to write grant bids for a non-profit group. Whatever your skills, there are likely groups that could benefit from your knowledge.

Spread Kindness

Acts of kindness can go a long way in making the world a better place. Consider paying for someone's meal in line behind you or leaving a nice note for a co-worker. Small acts can have a big effect and inspire others to do the same. No matter how you choose to give back, know that every act of kindness makes a difference. By finding ways to make a good effect, you can build a better world for yourself and those around you.

Giving Back Quotes & Inspiration for Generosity

As we think about the value of giving back, we turn to the knowledge of those who have championed this cause before us.

Here are some encouraging words to inspire charity and make a good effect on the world:

"No one has ever become poor by giving." – Anne Frank

These easy words tell us that giving back is not just about helping others, but also about improving our own lives and creating a more satisfying existence.

"The best way to find yourself is to lose yourself in the service of others." – Mahatma Gandhi

This quote speaks to the changing power of giving back – when we commit ourselves to helping others, we often find new strengths, interests, and a sense of purpose.

"We make a living by what we get, but we make a life by what we give." – Winston Churchill

This quote tells us that real success in life is not just about material wealth, but also about our effect on the world around us. When we value giving back, we build a sense of meaning and purpose that can support us for a lifetime.

"You can't live a perfect day without doing something for someone who will never be able to repay you." – John Wooden

This saying shows the importance of humility in our giving – real kindness is not about gaining credit or praise, but about doing good simply for the sake of helping others.

Take these words as motivation to give back, and explore the many ways in which you can make a good effect on the world around you.

The Ripple Effect of Giving Back: Impact Beyond the Individual

When we give back, the effect of our kindness goes far beyond ourselves. Acts of kindness and generosity can produce a rippling effect, inspiring others to do the same and building a culture of giving.

Impact on the Community

By giving back to our local society, we can have a good effect on the lives of those around us. Whether it's working at a community event, backing a local sports team, or making a gift to a charity, our actions can help to build a sense of unity and support within our community.

Moreover, the benefits of giving back to our community stretch beyond the instant effect. As we make good changes and inspire others to do the same, we can build a better and more resilient community for years to come.

The Power of Inspiration

One of the most important parts of giving back is the ability to inspire others. When we share our experiences and encourage others to get involved, we can create a ripple effect of giving that stretches far beyond ourselves.

Whether it's through social media, word of mouth, or simply showing by example, we can inspire others to take action and make a positive impact on the world. By sharing our love for giving back, we can help to build a more caring and helpful society.

Creating Lasting Change
Finally, giving back has the power to make real change on a big scale. By helping causes and groups that fit with our morals, we can help to drive progress in areas such as education, healthcare, and social justice.

Moreover, by inspiring others to get involved and supporting joint efforts, we can build a force for positive change that can have a permanent effect for generations to come.

Giving back is not just an act of kindness; it's a trigger for good change. By accepting our ability to make a difference in the lives of others and creating a culture of giving, we can build a better future for all.

Giving Back Activities: Creating Opportunities for Generosity

There are many ways to give back and have a good effect on your neighborhood and the world at large. By finding your ideals and hobbies, you can find chances to add acts of kindness into your daily life.

Here are some useful tips to help you get started:

1. Volunteering: Find a cause or group that fits with your values and hobbies, and look for work opportunities in your local neighborhood. Whether it's helping at a food bank, walking dogs at a shelter, or teaching children, there are countless ways to give your time and make a difference.

2. Giving: Consider giving money, goods, or services to charity groups that support issues you care about. Research reliable nonprofits to ensure your gift will have the biggest effect.

3. Supporting funding or advocacy efforts: Attend events, spread the word on social media, or join in fundraisers to support issues you care about. You can also write to your chosen leaders to fight for policies that match your ideals.

Remember, giving back doesn't have to be limited to traditional types of charity or work.

4. Random acts of kindness: Spread kindness and happiness by performing small acts of kindness for others, such as paying for a stranger's coffee, leaving a note of support, or holding the door open for someone.

5. Teaching: If you have information or skills that could benefit others, try teaching or coaching someone in your neighborhood. This can be a satisfying way to share your knowledge and help others achieve their goals.

6. Green initiatives: Help protect the environment by joining in neighborhood efforts to reduce trash, spare resources, and support sustainability. This could include working for a beach cleanup, planting trees, or starting a community farm.

By adding acts of kindness into your life, you can create a ripple effect of happiness and inspire others to do the same. Start small and remember that every act of kindness, no matter how small, can make a difference in someone's life.

Encouraging Generosity in the Workplace

Encouraging workers to give back is not only a way to support business social duty but it can also help to build a good workplace culture. When workers feel that their work is making a difference, it can lead to improved job happiness and employee retention.

Here are some ways to support kindness in the workplace:

1. Volunteer Programs

One way to support giving back at work is to organize volunteer programs that allow workers to give their time and skills to charity causes. This could involve a company-wide giving day or offering paid time off for workers to help in groups of their choice.

2. Donation Matching

Many businesses offer gift-matching programs where they will match employee payments to charity organizations. This can be a great way to incentivize staff to give back and can also help to improve the effect of business giving.

3. Charitable Initiatives

Another way to support giving back is to plan company-wide charity efforts, such as fundraising events or gift drives. This can help to build a sense of community within the workplace and can also help to raise knowledge about important issues.

4. Employee-Led Initiatives

Encouraging workers to lead their giving-back projects is another way to promote kindness in the workplace. This could involve helping employee-led projects, such as planning a charity run or starting a nonprofit fund within the company.

By creating a mindset of giving back at work, businesses can not only have a good effect on the community but also build a more interested and inspired workforce. Whether through volunteer programs, gift matches, charitable efforts, or employee-led projects, there are many ways to support kindness in the workplace.

The Joy of Giving Back

Many people find joy in giving back to their neighborhoods. Acts of kindness, big or small, can have a positive effect on others and leave a long memory on the person